The Secret

Mitōshi Akarui

Copyright © 2017 by Mitōshi Akarui

All rights reserved. No part of this publication may be reproduced, distributed, or transmitted in any form or by any means, including photocopying, recording, or other electronic or mechanical methods.

This is a work of fiction. Names, characters, businesses, places, events and incidents are either the products of the author's imagination or used in a fictitious manner. Any resemblance to actual persons, living or dead, or actual events is purely coincidental.

Contents

1. Which side of the waterline? 1
2. Vasco's treasure 9
3. And, to live… 15
4. A stone from my soul 27

"Despair has its own calms."

BRAM STROKER

1.

Which side of the waterline?

Giant, hideous, blood-thirsty butterflies were chasing me through a meadow strewn with rubies and emeralds. A fire-truck siren wailed in the background. I woke up.

9:32 am. I had been sleeping for 12 hours.

I checked my phone. 3 missed calls from Zoze. 1 missed call from Naina. 3 new messages. Who calls twice on a Sunday morning? I ignored the messages.

It was August 15, 2027 and there were two unsmoked joints on my nightstand. Freedom never felt so good.

Coffee was ready when I returned from the bathroom. I poured myself a cup and went to the balcony. A damp, rotten breeze from the Arabian Sea greeted me. I could hear the waves breaking against Fort Aguada's ramparts. It had stopped raining but the heat and humidity were unbearable. Mr. Gomes, the old man sitting in the opposite balcony, waved a tricolor at me and shouted "Hey Francis, waking up late on Independence Day? Looks like you've been partying hard, no?" I threw back a dishonest smile. "Jerk", I thought, "Bloody mosquito of a neighbor." I stubbed my cigarette, wiped the sweat off my forehead and retreated to the air-conditioned comfort of my apartment. India had solved every problem except oppressive heat and intrusive neighbors.

I poured another cup of coffee, sat on the sofa and lit another cigarette. I turned the television on. The Prime Minister was addressing the nation.

"....in the last 10 years the Government of India has completed the program. We have finally redeemed the pledge to our people. It took 80 long years, fortitude and fortune for India to succeed in its endeavor...

Fighter jets flew past.

...to bring freedom and opportunity to the common man, to the peasants and workers of India; to fight and end poverty and ignorance and disease; to build up a prosperous, democratic and progressive nation, and to create social, economic and political institutions which will ensure justice and fullness of life to every man and woman."

Applause.

"...The war with China, precipitated by that country's seizure of our beloved Ching-La heights, has left no visible scars upon the republic..."

I agreed. The temporary occupation of Sikkim by the invading Peoples Liberation Army of China had been forgotten in the joy over repeated victories in Tibet, and the subsequent trouncing of PLA along the entire North-Eastern border.

"...The Bangladesh and Myanmar acquisitions have paid off strategically and the territory of Sri Lanka has developed as a global commerce, finance and transport hub."

He did not add that Kashmir was no longer a problem. After the implosion of Pakistan, that country had been carved into three spheres of influence with India retaining control over fertile Punjab and Sindh provinces, Afghanistan controlling the poppy and AK-47 rich mountainous northwest

Khyber; and Iran in charge of its south-western part Balochistan.

> "....*my fellow countrymen, today our nation is prosperous, connected and epidemic free.....We are a global superpower, the most powerful nation in history. An ancient civilization restored to its past glory.*"

Indeed. This was supposed to be China's century after America had abdicated its superpower throne and had walled itself into a cocoon by withdrawing from all international trade and military treaties to deal with its opioid epidemic and civil wars. But a discovery of massive reserves of lithium deposits in Thar Desert coupled with a robust program to create millions of solar energy farms tipped the balance in India's favor. We were no longer dependent on oil and gas rich nations. The obsolescence of internal combustion engine had thrown Russia, America and the middle-east into recession. China coveted our lithium. They failed in their endeavors, miserably. We had profited well by the latest treaties with United Europe which now headquartered most global corporate giants outside India.

When the Government solved the Maoist problem and squadrons of Maoist rebels in ragtag gear crawled out of the forests and surrendered to the Minister of Internal Affairs, the nation drew a long sigh of relief. After the United Nations Compact on Religions, bigotry and intolerance were burnt on their pyres and kindness and charity began to draw warring religions, castes and sects together. When India led the permanent destruction of global nuclear stockpile many believed our country had finally arrived, at least in the new world which after all is a world by itself.

But self-preservation is the first law, and India had to look on in helpless sorrow as Japan, Korea, Thailand and

Singapore writhed in the throes of anarchy, while China pounced and bound them one by one.

> "....and today I have an important announcement to make," the prime minister continued. I turned the volume up. "The Ministry of Health has recommended and I have approved declaration of countrywide emergency to counter anemia related deaths in our country. My fellow citizens, despite all the progress that we have made during last ten years, we have not been able to prevent the disturbingly high rate of anemia fatalities in our country. What started out as an outlier event in one hilly state has now become an epidemic, the like of which we have never seen before. My friends, today this is the single largest threat facing our people, and our country. But I am confident that with a concerted effort we will counter and slay this demon."

!!!

> ".....And to India, our much-loved motherland, the ancient, the eternal and the ever-new, we pay our reverent homage and we bind ourselves afresh to her service. JAI HIND," he concluded.

National Anthem followed.

My heart started pounding and blood rushed to my ears as I repeated to myself:

> "...But I am confident that with a concerted effort we will counter and slay this demon."

...Bharata-bhagya-vidhata...

"We need to do something about it," I thought, "and fast."

...uchchala-jaladhi-taranga...

"If we don't, this beast, anemia, will annihilate our country, and also possibly wipe human civilization off the face of earth. I need to talk to Professor D'Costa, right now!"

...gahe tava jaya-gatha.

I didn't wait for the National Anthem to conclude before I turned the television off and reached for the phone.

Professor D'Costa answered after eight rings.

"Hello..." he sounded distracted. In the background I could hear electronic beeps and human moans. The servers... "What's up, Francis?"

"Professor, did you hear the prime minister's announcement?" I enquired.

"No, something significant?" he asked.

"Yes, the government has declared emergency to counter anemia in the country."

"Oh!" he exclaimed.

"Yes," I agreed; and then asked, "What are we going to do about it?

"Hey, take it easy. Let me think."

"Then think fast, we don't have much time."

"Okay, we can activate our plan tonight. Everything is ready. I need to go over the plan...easy, bitch mind you teeth...no, that was not for you. Yeah, I mean let's do it tonight. Can you take the next flight to New Delhi?"

"Yes." I replied.

"OK, then. We can drive together to Naggar tonight."

"Will we find them?" I expressed my doubt.

"Absolutely." The Professor assured me.

"Fine. See you then."

"See you."

I ended the call and logged into a travel booking site. Yes, tickets were available for a late afternoon flight.

"...we can activate our plan tonight." The mere thought felt like drawing out a sword from its scabbard. "This is it!" I determined, and clicked the buy now button.

It was quarter past ten. I was hungry, and trembling with excitement. I took two bread slices and put them in the toaster. Nothing calms me like browned toast with a thick layer of butter.

As I was sitting down to eat, I looked at Naina's picture, and the envelope that contained the fateful letter from Zoze. Now that it was going to be all over, it seemed like a bad dream. But when I looked at Naina's picture again, I realized it couldn't have been a dream. Actually, it was only six months ago that I had sat at this same desk, looking at her picture, wondering what could have happened to her. That night I had tried a brand new cocktail of mind altering enablers. I don't remember what happened after the sixth joint.

The overdose incident had left no lasting results despite the doctors' fears that there could be long term effects on my mental capabilities; on the contrary it had changed me for the better. From a university drop-out, I had become active, energetic, and fiercely ambitious. The only thing that troubled me was when people questioned reality —*My reality*.

During my time at the government de-addiction clinic, I had read for the first time, *Rooh Ka Darinda*. I remember after finishing the first chapter that it occurred to me that I should stop reading it. I threw the book away; it struck the wall and fell open on the floor under the lampshade. I bent to pick it up and my eyes caught the open page. I got a glimpse of the opening words in the second chapter. With a cry of terror, or perhaps it was of joy, I picked the book up and crept shaking to my chair. I read it and reread it, and cried and laughed and trembled with a horror which still affects me. This is the thing that troubles me. This is reality and they call it distorted reality. Some call it hallucinations.

I cannot forget Mount Gandhamadana where golden stars emerge from the lake on the summit; where the reflections of men's desires take the shape of red anemones; where rubies and emeralds litter the landscape, when the twin rainbows cross each other in green skies; and my mind will bear forever the memory of the soul monster's mask.

I know God will curse the writer, as the writer has cursed the world with this magical, magnificent creation, terribly simple yet irresistibly true. The world now trembles before *Rooh ka Darinda.* When the Swedish Government seized the copies which had just arrived in Stockholm, Copenhagen, of course, became eager to read it. The book spread like an epidemic, from city to city, from continent to continent, banned by governments, confiscated by police, burnt by religious leaders, deleted and denounced by the literary community. Websites and social media posts linking to the soft copies popped overnight. A monster had been unleashed. No force was big enough to stop this juggernaut. No fire hose was big enough to douse the fire that had been lit.

It is certain that no principles of humanity had been violated in those wicked pages, no physical laws had been challenged and no values, modern or traditional, had been outraged. It could not be judged by any known standards, although it was universally accepted that the supreme note of art had been struck in *Rooh Ka Darinda*. The words hid the essence of pure poison and human nature could not bear the strain. The innocence of the first chapter allowed the horrific blow to fall afterward with awful consequences.

Rooh Ka Darinda was the only known text in the world that dealt with the art and science of exorcism. Nobody had ever claimed authorship of this magnificent manual.

I needed a deep-soaking, relaxing bath. I filled the bathtub, turned on Beethoven's *Ode to Joy*, lit a joint and entered the tub. I wanted to read Zoze's letter again. The cold water was like a curtain separating reality and dreams.

Not many people realized which side of the curtain they belonged.

2.

Vasco's treasure

It had been six weeks since there had been any word from Naina, and she had promised to call as soon as she reached Manali. Considering that my future rested in her hands, I had every right to be apprehensive.

We had grown up together, had lost our parents within a few years of each other and had been fond of each other the way kids are apt to be. Then the change came: It seemed I loved her, and she was still just "fond" of me. During our early college days in Panjim I sort of let things ride, but once we went on to Goa University, I began to find opportunities to spend more time with her.

The next thing I knew, she had signed up with a student tour destined for Manali & Leh, and told me she would give me my answer when she returned. I had to be content with that, but couldn't help worrying. Naina was a strange girl—withdrawn, dreamy and soft-hearted. Knowing the section she was going to, I was inclined to be uneasy, since it is the realm of marijuana addicts, fortune tellers and the like. It is also the birthplace of many strange legends, and Naina claimed to be strongly psychic. As a matter of fact, she had foretold one or two things which were probably coincidental, like the death of our parents, and which even made an impression on me—and you'd hardly call me a "believer."

This so-called talent of hers led her into trouble on more than one occasion. I remember in her final year at college she fell under the spell of a short, fat, astrologer with a strictly phony accent until I realized something was amiss, got to the bottom of it, and dispatched friend astrologer pronto. If she should meet some unscrupulous person now, with no one around to get her out of the scrape—but I didn't want to think of that. I was sure this time everything would be all right.

When she didn't call at first, I let it go that she was busy. My call always went to her voicemail. She didn't reply to any of my emails or text messages. Finally, six weeks' silent treatment aroused my curiosity and fear. It also aroused my nasty temper, and the next thing I knew I was in a flight to Manali. Within four hours after reaching Manali, with the help of local police, I found her at a little holiday cottage, a quaint little place that looked as if it were made of firewood, and was surrounded by the huge, craggy Himalayan mountain range. I also found Zoze Silveira.

"What's wrong, Naina? Why didn't you ever call back?" I asked.

Her usually happy, shining black eyes flashed angrily. "Why couldn't you leave me alone? I told you not to come after me. I came here so I could think this out. For God's sake, Francis, can't you see I wanted to think? To be by myself?"

"But you promised to call," I persisted, wondering at this change in her, this impatience. Wondered, too, at her wraithlike slimness. She'd always been curved in the right places.

"Naina has been studying much too diligently," Zoze said slowly. "She's always tired lately. She hasn't been too well, either. Her throat bothers her."

I wanted to punch his head in. For some reason I didn't like him. Not because I sensed his rivalry; I was above that.

God knows I wanted her to be happy, above everything. It was just something about him that irritated me. An attitude. Not supercilious; I could have coped with that. Rather, it was a calm imperturbability that seemed to speak his faith in his eventual success, regardless of any effort on my part.

I don't know how to fight that sort of strategy. I look like I am: blunt and obvious. Suddenly I didn't care if he was there.

"Naina. Naina, dear. This guy's no good for you, can't you see that? What do you know about him?"

She looked at me, her eyes surprised and a little hurt. Then she looked at him, seemed to be looking through him and into herself, if you know what I mean. A slow flush spread from the base of her throat, that thin, almost transparent throat.

"All I have to know," she said softly. "I love him."

She looked out the window. "I'm going up to Naggar, to a small monastery for my health shortly; the doctor has told me I must go away, and Zoze has suggested this place. There Zoze and I shall be married."

I knew then how it felt to be on the receiving end of a monkey-punch. That she had come to this decision because of my objections, I had not the slightest doubt. She was going to marry someone about whom she knew absolutely nothing. She was much more ill than she knew. Zoze was undoubtedly after her money; she was considerably well-off. Obviously she was once more being influenced in the wrong direction.

"I won't let you!" I warned. "Give it some more time, if for nothing else, then for old times' sake."

"How about me, Francis?" Zoze interrupted. "You haven't asked me my feelings on the subject. I happen to love

Naina dearly. Have I no say just because you're a childhood friend of hers?"

"Childhood friend! I was her whole family for years before she ever heard of you! I'll see you in hell before I let her marry you!" I shouted. Looking back, I'm sure that had he said anything else, I would have killed him, if Naina hadn't come between us.

"That's enough, Francis! I've heard all I want to from you. I'm twenty-three, and if I choose to marry Zoze, I'll do so and there's nothing you can do about it. Now, please go."

"Okay, Naina," I said, "if that's the way you want it. But I'm not through. If you won't protect yourself, I'll do it for you. I'd like to know more about the mysterious Mr. Zoze Silveira, and I do wish, for your own sake, you'd do the same. I wouldn't care if you married Vasco Da Gama, so long as you knew all about him. People just don't marry strangers; not if they're smart. For God's sake, ask him about himself!"

"All right, Francis," she replied, smiling patiently. "I'll ask him. Now, do stop being childish."

"Okay, darling," I said sheepishly. "But do me one more favor. Don't marry him until I get back. Only a little while; give me a week. Just wait a little longer."

As I closed the door, I could still feel his smile, mocking—yet a little sad.

But Naina didn't wait. I was gone a week. I had worn down online search engines trying to track down the elusive Mister Silveira and discovered exactly—nothing. I did find his address and all his landlady could tell me was that he was a Goan who had come to this climate for his health, and that he slept late mornings. I was licked and I knew it. If I had been a pup, I would have fitted my tail neatly between my legs and made for home. But I wasn't a pup, so I headed straight for Naina's flat to face the music.

They were waiting for me, she and Zoze. When I saw her, I wished I were dead.

She lay in Zoze's arms, her body a mere whisper of a body. White and cold she was, like frozen milk on a cold winter's day. They were both dead.

You know how it is when at a funeral someone views the deceased and says kindly, "She's beautiful," and "she" isn't beautiful at all; just a made-up, lifeless handful of clay. Dead as dead, and frightening. Well, it wasn't that way this time. Their skins were extremely pale and their dark heads, hers black and his deep brown, gleamed brightly. And they sat so close in the sofa before next to the window, his head resting in the hollow of her throat. They looked—peaceful; no line marred their faces. I almost fancied I saw them breathe. And on her third finger, left hand, was the ring—a thin, platinum band. He had won, and in winning somehow he had lost. How they had died and why they found each other and death at the same time, I would probably never know. I only knew one thing: I had to get away from there—quickly. I almost ran the distance to my flat. Stumbled into the place and poured a triple Scotch which I could scarcely hold. The Scotch seared my throat and tasted bitter; someone must have poured salt in it. Then I realized that it was tears—my tears. I, Francis Coelho, who hadn't cried since my fifth birthday—I was sobbing like a baby.

I didn't call the police. That would mean I would have to go back and watch them cover that lovely body, carry it away and submit it to untold indignities in order to ascertain the cause of death. The maid would find them in the morning and would notify the police.

But it wasn't as simple as that. In the morning I found I couldn't shake off the guilt which possessed me. Even two bottles of Scotch hadn't helped me to forget. I was dead drunk and cold sober at the same time.

I phoned Naina's landlady and told her I had failed to reach her by phone, that I was sure something was amiss. Would she please go to their flat and see if anything was wrong.

She was amused. "Really, Mr. Coelho, you must be mistaken. Naina went out just an hour ago with her new husband. Surely you are jesting. Why she has never looked better. So happy. They have left for Naggar. They have also left you a note.

I told her I would be right over, and hopped a cab. I began to think I was losing my mind. I had seen them both—dead. The landlady had seen them this morning—alive!"

3.

And, to live…

When I could no longer hold my breath under water I got out. I picked the envelope from the desk, pulled the letter out and ran my wet fingers over the crease. I doubted that I had ever read it at all—but the blue ink on the white paper forced me to acknowledge its reality. It had been written by Zoze, in a neat, scholar's script.

Dear Francis: (It began)

Why should I not have wanted Naina? You did; others doubtless did. Why then should she not be mine? There are many things worse than being married to me; she might have married a man who beat her!

With her I have known the two happiest days of my life. I want no more than that. I have no right to ask for more. Have we, any of us, a right to endless bliss on this earth? Hardly. You thought of her welfare above all; for that I owe you some explanation. You must be patient, you must believe, and in the end, you must do as I ask. You must.

You wanted to know about me—of my life before Naina. Before Naina? It seems strange to think about it. There is no life without Naina. Still, there was a time when for me she didn't exist. I have been constantly going forward to the day when I would meet her, yet there was a time when I didn't know where I would find her, or even what her name would be!

It was chance that brought us together. For me, good chance; for you, possibly ill chance; for Naina? Only she can say. Some three years ago I was studying in New Delhi. The future held great things for me. I was a Goan like yourself, and damn proud of it. Life in New Delhi seemed strange and slow and sometimes utterly dismal. Then, little by little I slipped into their slower ways, growing to love the people for their brashness, and finally coming to feel I was one of them, so to speak.

I have said everything slowed down: I was wrong. Studying intensified for me. The folklore of exiled Tibetans intrigued me. I delved into the mountain tales, the mischievous fancies of the mountain men, the legends of the yeti. For me it was a relief from political science, which suddenly palled and which smacked of treason in the light of current events. My extracurricular research consumed the better part of my evenings. My books were and always have been a part of me, and as was to be expected, I overdid it. I studied too hard with too little let-up. Sometimes it seemed to me there was more truth to what I read than myth. It became somewhat of an obsession. Suddenly, one night, everything blacked out.

I came to in a rehabilitation center. I didn't know how I got there, and when they explained it to me, I laughed. I thought they were joking. When I tried to get up, to walk, I collapsed. Then I knew how bad it had been. I knew, too, I would have to go slowly.

It was there I met Livia. She was beautiful. Not like Naina, who is like a fragile, fair, spun-sugar angel. Livia was more earthy, with skin like ivory, creamy and rich and pale. Her blue-black hair she wore long and gathered in the back. She looked about twenty-five, but a streak of pure white ran back from each of her temples. She was the most striking woman I have ever met. I had never known anyone like her, nor have I since I saw her last.

You know how it is: the air of mystery about a woman makes a man like a kid again. She reminded me of a sleek, black cat, with her large, hazel eyes. I bumped into her one day on the verandah, and spent every day with her after that.

The doctors wanted me to take exercise—short walks and the like, and Livia went with me, struggling to keep up with me. The slightest effort tired her. She suffered from a rather nasty case of anemia. She seldom smiled; the effort was probably too much for her. I saw her really smile only once.

We had been on one of our short hikes in the woods close by the grounds. She stumbled over a twig or a branch, I'm not sure which. Suddenly she was in my arms. Have you ever held a cloud in your arms, Francis? So light she was, although she was almost as tall as I. Warm and pulsating. Her eyes held mine; it was almost uncanny. I have never been affected like that by a woman. Then I was kissing her; then a sharp sting, and I winced. There was the warm, salt taste of blood on my lips. I never knew how it happened. But she was smiling, her full mouth parted in the strangest smile I have ever seen. And those small white teeth gleamed; and in her eyes, which were all black pupils now, with the iris quite hidden, was desire—or something beyond desire. I couldn't define it then; now, I think I can. Her small, pink tongue darted over her lips, tasting, seeming to savor.

I was frightened, for some indefinable reason. I wanted to get away from her, from the woods, from myself. I grasped her arm roughly and we started back for the grounds. We never mentioned the episode again, but we neither of us ever forgot. She intrigued me now, more than ever. The doctors were able to satisfy my curiosity somewhat. They told me she had been a patient for some four years. Some days she was better, some days worse. She needed rest—much rest. Most days she slept past noon with their approval. Some days there was a faint flush beneath that ivory skin; other days it was pale and cool.

Just when we became lovers, I scarcely remember. Things were happening so fast I could barely keep pace with them. There was a magnetism about Livia which compelled. I couldn't have resisted if I'd wanted to—and I didn't.

I began to have long periods of fatigue, times when I would black out and remember nothing afterwards. And the dreams began. I would dream I was stroking a large, velvety-black cat, a cat with shining yellow eyes that looked at me as if they knew my every thought. I would stroke it continuously and it would nip me playfully. Then, one night the dream intensified: I was playing with the creature, caressing it gently, when of a sudden its lips drew back in a snarl, and without warning it sprang at my throat and buried its fangs deep! I thought I could feel life being drawn from me; I screamed.

The doctors told me afterwards that I was semi-conscious for days; that I had to be restrained.

When I was well again, Livia came to see me. She was gentle—soothing. She held me close to her and oh! it was good to be alive and to belong to someone.

I remember to this day what she wore. Black velvet lounging slacks, a low-necked amber satin blouse, caught at the "V" by a curiously wrought antique silver pin. It was round, about four inches in diameter. In its center was the carved figure of a serpent coiled to strike. Its eyes were deep amber topazes and its darting tongue was raised and set with a blood-red ruby.

"What an unusual pin, Livia," I said "I've never seen it before, have I?"

"No," she replied. "It belongs to the deep, dark, seldom discussed skeleton in the D'Mello closet, Zoze. You see, my great-great grandmother was quite a wicked lady, to hear tell. Went in for Witches' masses and the like. They say she poisoned her husband, a rather elderly and very childish man, for her lover, whom she subsequently married. Together they did away with relatives who stood in the way of their accumulating more money. This pin was the instrument of death."

Her slim fingers pressed the ruby tongue and the pin opened, revealing a space large enough to secrete powder. "It's like those employed by the infamous Saldanhas, as you can see," she continued, shrugging. "Perhaps it was fate then, that her devoted new husband tired of her once her fortune was assured him, took a young mistress for himself, and disposed of the unfortunate wife, using her own pin to perpetrate her murder. She was excommunicated by her church, too, which must have made it most unpleasant for her, poor old dear." The slim shoulders straightened. "But let's not discuss such unpleasant things, my dear. The important thing now is for you to get well quickly. I've missed you terribly, you know."

It was then I asked her to marry me. I knew I didn't really love her, but there seemed nothing to prevent our marriage. And she had gotten under my skin. It was as elemental as that. She said she thought we should wait until I fully recovered.

"Don't say any more, darling," she said. "Rest your poor, sore throat."

She bent over me solicitously and I reached up to stroke that smooth black hair. It had a familiar feel to it that I couldn't quite place. Of course I had stroked it hundreds of times before, but it wasn't that. Then she looked straight at *me, those large, glowing hazel eyes boring into mine, and I knew. Knew and disbelieved at the same time. I froze where I lay, paralyzed by my fear; unable to make a sound.*

"So you know," she whispered. "It is well. I have marked you for my own these many months. Now that you know, you will not fight. You know what I am, or at least you can guess. This pin you admired so—it was mine three hundred years ago and it will always be mine!"

Her lips were on mine. She had never kissed me like this. It was like the touch of hot ice, freezing, then searing. Unendurable. I lay inert; I couldn't have moved if I wanted to. I could scarcely breathe. Then I felt the blood within me pounding, pulsing, beginning to answer in spite of myself. I tasted once more the warm, salty fluid on my lips. Livia's body was liquid in my arms; warm, heady, narcotizing. Once again I felt the agonizing, dagger sharp pain in my throat and—darkness.

Have you ever wakened to a bright, sunny afternoon and heard yourself pronounced dead? They spoke in low, hushed tones. How unfortunate. Young fellow only thirty, dying so far away from his homeland. No family. Good thing he was well-set in life. This sudden anemia was most extraordinary; fellow showed no signs of it previously. All he had really needed was rest. If he had recovered, that lovely Livia D'Mello might have made both their lives happier, richer. Sad ending to what might have been an idyll. Good of her to claim the body. She said she was going to inter it in the family vault in Naggar.

I heard them distinctly. I wanted to shout that I wasn't dead; I wanted to wake up from this horrible nightmare. I was as alive as they. I knew I had to get out of there, some way; to get away from Livia, whom I now feared. They left to make arrangements.

The fatigue crept through me without warning; I dozed in spite of myself. And I dreamed again. I was a cat running, leaping through windows, loping over the countryside, stopping for no one. I panted with my exertions. Towns and cities flew by; I had to get someplace and quickly. Then the dream ended.

"Zoze," she said, "Get up, my dear." I heard her and I hated her. Hated her while I was drawn to her. There was a white mist before my eyes. I reached up to brush it away. It was not a mist; it was a cloth. I shivered.

"I must wake up," I whispered hoarsely, "I must! I'm going mad!" There was a creaking sound and daylight descended upon me. When I saw where I was, I covered my face with my hands and sobbed. I tried to pray, but the words froze on my lips. I was sitting in a coffin in a mausoleum! I had been buried alive!

"What am I?" I shrieked. "Where am I and what have you done? I'm out of my mind; stark, staring mad!" Livia's lips parted, showing the even white teeth—those slightly pointed teeth. "You're quite sane, my dear," She said calmly. "You are now one of us; a revenant, even as I, and to live you must feed on the living." "It's not true!" I shouted. "This is all a crazy nightmare, part of my illness! You're not real! Nothing is real!"

"I'm quite real, Zoze. To be trite, I am what I am, and have accepted it calmly, as you shall in time. I have told you of my life. You have been a student of legends. Legends are often—more often than you think—reality. When one has been murdered, if one has lived a so-called wicked life, he is doomed to walk the earth battening on the living. My fate was sealed as I lay in my coffin. But that wasn't enough. As I lay there, my pet cat, Zuma, slunk into the room and leapt over me. That was a double insurance of my life after death.

Those whom I mark for my own must, too, live on. Accept it, my dear. You have no other choice."

"No!" I cried. "I'm religious! Things like this don't happen to us! It's only in stories, movies and nightmares!"

She chuckled drily. "I'm afraid these things do happen, and in this case, you're it, my dear. Make the best of it."

But I wouldn't; I refused to—for a while. I would not feast on the blood of the living. Something within me fought. For a time.

Then, the awful hunger began. The tearing pangs of hunger that ordinary food wouldn't arrest. I fought it as long as I could. I lost.

First it was small animals; animals that I loved. It was my life or theirs. Then there was a little girl; a dear little creature who might have been my child under different circumstances. After the episode of the little girl, Livia left me. She had no further use for me; she had wanted the child, too, and I had got it. I was now competition to be shunned. I was alone once again alone and thoroughly miserable. I couldn't understand myself, my motives, so how could I expect someone else to understand?

I only knew what I was; nor could I rationalize on why I had become this way. I could only presume it had happened to others equally as innocent as myself of wrong-doing. In the daytime, when I was like others, I reproached myself; goodness knows I loathed myself and what I had to do in order to "live." I wished I might really die, for I was tired—so frightfully tired and sick of it all. But I knew of no way to accomplish this, so I had to bear it all, fasting until my voracious, disgusting appetites got the better of me.

I decided there must be some information on my kind, particularly in this area where vampire legends are rife, so I took to haunting reading rooms. It was there I met Naina.

She told me, after we knew each other better, that she was doing graduate work in regional superstitions and had decided that her thesis would treat of the history of vampirism. She found it terribly amusing, but at the same time frightening: Didn't I? I fear I saw nothing laughable about it, but I held my peace. Why, I could have done a thesis for her that would have driven some mild-mannered prof completely out of his mind! I kept my knowledge to myself, though; I didn't want to scare Naina.

She was like a flash of sunshine in a darkened room. She made each day worth living. For the first time the hunger pangs ceased. Ceased for one week, then two. I was certain I was cured. Perhaps, I thought, the whole thing was just a dream and I am finally awake.

I felt then I had the right to tell her of my love. She looked infinitely sad. She wasn't certain, she said. She knew she was awfully fond of me, but she was confused. She had just come away from Goa, trying to make up her mind about someone dear, whom she didn't want to hurt, and she wanted a breather. I said I would wait up to and through eternity, if she wished.

Things went along peacefully then. We would walk for hours together, walk in complete silence and understanding. My strength seemed to be returning more day by day. We went far afield in search of material for her thesis. She would track down the most minute speck of hearsay, to get authenticity.

One day, in our wanderings, I thoughtlessly let myself be led too near my resting place. One of the locals mentioned a "place of horror" nearby and Naina wanted to investigate. I had no choice. We poked amid the still fustiness of the deserted mausoleum I knew so well. She thought it odd that the door was unlocked. I said, yes, wasn't it. Then she saw the box, that gleaming copper box which Livia had so thoughtfully provided. She stroked it gently, commenting on its beauty, and before I could prevent it or divert her attention, she had lifted the heavy lid exposing the disarranged shroud, the remains of one or two hapless small creatures, the horrible blood-stained satin lining. She screamed and dropped the lid, somehow pinching her finger. She hopped on one foot, as one usually does to fight down sudden pain. Then she was clinging to me, thoroughly frightened.

"What does it mean, Zoze?"

I quieted her with the usual platitudes. Then I was kissing that poor, red little finger. Without warning to myself or her, I nipped it affectionately. A warm glow spread through me; there was a taste more delightful than fine old brandy, or vintage wine, and I knew irrevocably that I was not cured; no, nor ever should be! And I knew, too, that I wanted Naina—not just as a man longs for the woman he loves—but to drink of the fountain of her life, that warm, intoxicating fountain, greedily, joyously. She never knew what went through my mind at that moment. If I could have killed myself then, I would have, and with no compunction. But there is more to killing a revenant than that. The Church knows the procedure. I hurried Naina home as fast as I could and told her I had to go away for a week on business. She believed me and said she would miss me. But I didn't go away. That night I fought a losing battle with myself, and then and every night thereafter, I returned to her, partook of her and slunk away, loathing myself. I knew that I must soon kill the one being I loved above all others, kill, too, her immortal soul, and there was nothing I could do to prevent it.

She began to fade visibly. When I "returned" in a week, she was so ill that a few steps tired her. Her appetite all but vanished. She seemed genuinely glad to see me. She was beset by nightmares, she said. Could I help her get some rest? I took her to a physician who sagely prescribed a change in climate, rest and a diet rich in blood and iron, gave her a prescription for sedatives, and called it a day.

You know how she looked when you saw her. The day was approaching when she would have no more blood, when life as you know it would stop and she would become like me. Somehow I couldn't take her with me without some warning, but I didn't know how to do it. You see, since I was an innocent victim myself, I could speak, could warn my intended victim, because although my soul had all but died, there was still a spark that evil hadn't touched. I knew she would think it a joke if I told her about myself without warning.

Then, happily for me, you came along. I knew you would sense something amiss and I didn't care. I was almost certain of her love, and I decided to seize the few minutes left me and devil take the hindmost! When you told her to confront me, you gave me the happiest days of my life. For this I thank you sincerely. For what I have done and will ask you to do, forgive me!

Naina asked me directly, as you had known she would. I replied frankly, sparing her nothing. I told her that the fact that this life had been wished on me, as it were, gave me some rights, and that I could tell her how to rid herself of me, if she wished. Then she turned to me, her large, lovely eyes thoughtful.

"Zoze, dearest," she said softly, "I must die some day, really die, so what difference does it make when? I only know that I love you. Why wait until I'm decrepit and alone, with only a few memories to look back on? Why not now, with you, where life doesn't really stop? With all I've read about this, don't you think I could free myself if I wished?"

I still wonder if she really believed me. We were married three days later. I never told her what her life with me would be like—that one day I would desert her, fearing and hating her rivalry for the very source of my life, and the ghastly chain would continue. I couldn't. I loved her so, Francis, can you understand that? I couldn't betray her then and I can't now.

On the second night of our marriage, she died as you know it, in my arms. I don't think she knows it yet. But it won't be long until she does discover it. We were quite alive when you found us; she was in an hypnotic state induced by her condition. She heard and saw nothing. But I knew. And I must keep my faith. I must, and you are the only one who can help me.

If you will show this to a priest, or someone with a deep understanding of vampirism he will gladly accompany you to the place in Naggar, where we rest during the morning in a new "bed" I had specially constructed for us. I couldn't bring Naina to that other bed of corruption. A map of how to get there is enclosed. There you will perform the ancient, effective rites, and you will lay us to rest together, as we wish. That is all I ask....

That's where the letter ended.

I stared at nothing, trying to force myself to think. In substance, he wished me to murder the girl I loved. I could refuse; I could ignore his request. I could even doubt the veracity of his statements. He might be a madman. But I didn't doubt. I believed every word, and I knew I would do as he asked. That she had gone willingly I didn't doubt. I no longer hated him so much; rather I pitied him, the hapless victim of a horrible chain of circumstance.

4.

A stone from my soul

The flight from Dabolim Airport to New Delhi was uneventful. I took the metro train to Hauz Khas station. Kalu Sarai, tucked behind the metro station, is a medieval era catacomb of lanes and bylanes. The maze of tenements is built like a three-dimensional nightmare of lego bricks created by an unimaginative four year old. This is where dreamers and drifters came, and this is where I had found Professor D'Costa when I discovered that he was the true author of *Rooh Ka Darinda*. He never admitted.

Professor D'Costa was a venerable, gentle soul. When I had first shown him Zoze's letter he had looked at me searchingly, laughed and told me to read the Good Book for consolation, and to lay off the bottle. Professor D'Costa was understanding, with the wisdom of the very old.

"Yes, my son," he had said, "I will go. Many might doubt, but I believe. Lucifer roams the earth in many guises and must be recognized and exorcised."

The professor answered the doorbell and let me in. We ate a simple dinner of curry rice and set off for Naggar. We drove through the night and it was five o'clock in the morning when we approached the mausoleum. He explained that the "creatures of darkness" had to be back in their resting places before the cock crew. At night they drew sustenance; during the morning they slept.

There was a gleaming copper casket. Zoze had not lied. We approached it warily. In it was nothing but grisly remains, bloodstains and dust. We drew back, fearful. Then we saw the other, newer casket in richest mahogany, almost twice the width of the copper box: Their bridal bed!

They lay together, his arm about her. She wore a gown of palest blue, but oh, that mockery of a gown! Stained it was with fresh blood which had seeped onto it from him. Obviously she had not taken to prowling yet. His mouth was dark, rich with blood, slightly open in a half-smile. His hand pressed her fair head close to his chest. She lay trustingly within the circle of his arm, like a small child. Professor D'Costa crossed himself. The bodies twitched slightly.

"You know what you must do," he whispered.

I nodded, the pit of my stomach churning madly. I couldn't do it! Not Naina, the lovely. But I knew I would; I had to. She must not wake again to see that blood-stained gown or to wonder at her husband's gory lips. She should know rest, eternal rest.

Professor D'Costa circled the box several times, ringing a small bell, and at one point laid a crucifix upon each of their chests. Their faces writhed and I felt my skin creep.

Then, chanting in a low, firm voice, he gave me the signal. Together we drove two long stakes, dipped first in Holy Water, home, piercing their hearts simultaneously.

The bodies leapt forward in the box, straining against the stake, and a horrible, drawn-out wail shattered the stillness of the tomb. Professor D'Costa dropped to his knees and I clapped my hands over my ears, but the dreadful shriek penetrated. My stomach turned over and I retched. The professor followed suit. We were no supermen and our bodies and our very souls revolted against this monstrous thing.

"Let us finish, Francis," the professor said slowly, after a time, his face the color of ashes. "We must bury these dead, that they may sleep in consecrated ground."

I couldn't. I had to see her again before it was done. She lay, small and fragile as ever, her face calm, only there was no trace of life now. She was still and white, as only the dead—the truly dead—are. Zoze's arm was flung across her chest, as if to protect her. I made myself move the arm, resting her head upon his shoulder, where it belonged. Then, as I looked, there was just Naina. Zoze was gone and only a handful of dust lay piled up around the stake. It was enough. I slammed the lid shut.

***

Looking back now, I can see it was all for the best. Naina was different—apart from other women. A dreamer, a mystic, too easily influenced by the bizarre and un-normal. I, on the other hand, am practical almost to a fault. Had she married me I might have crushed in her the very thing that drew me to her. In time she might have grown to hate me.

Zoze, on the other hand, was a student. Introspective, given to romanticizing. Susceptible to suggestion. Had I been confronted with a Livia, I should have run like hell. To him, though, she was cloaked in mystery; hence, more desirable. What better choice for him ultimately than Naina? That Naina had to die to achieve her happiness is of no real importance. Life is a transitory thing anyway.

Sometimes, though, when I look at Naina's picture, it's hard to be practical. She was everything I shall ever want.

I had never been to Manali before the summer of 2027. I went to find Naina, to marry her. Instead, I found and murdered her, and I will never go back again.

THE END

www.ingramcontent.com/pod-product-compliance
Lightning Source LLC
Chambersburg PA
CBHW021454080526
44588CB00009B/850